THE HOLOCAUST

Life and Death in the Camps

Jane Shuter

H www.heinemann.co.uk/library
Visit our website to find out more information about **Heinemann Library** books.

To order:
☎ Phone 44 (0) 1865 888066
🖹 Send a fax to 44 (0) 1865 314091
💻 Visit the Heinemann Bookshop at www.heinemann.co.uk/library to browse our catalogue and order online.

First published in Great Britain by Heinemann Library, Halley Court, Jordan Hill, Oxford OX2 8EJ, part of Harcourt Education. Heinemann is a registered trademark of Harcourt Education Ltd.

Editorial: Andrew Farrow and Georga Godwin
Design: Joanna Sapwell and Tinstar Design (www.tinstar.co.uk)
Illustrations: Martin Griffin
Picture Research: Maria Joannou and Thelma Gilbert
Production: Viv Hichens

Originated by Ambassador Litho Ltd
Printed in Hong Kong by Wing King Tong

ISBN 0 431 15363 9 (hardback)
06 05 04 03
10 9 8 7 6 5 4 3 2

ISBN 0 431 15368 X (paperback)
07 06 05 04 03
10 9 8 7 6 5 4 3 2 1

British Library Cataloguing in Publication Data

Shuter, Jane
The Holocaust: Life and Death in the Camps
940.5'318
A full catalogue record for this book is available from the British Library.

Acknowledgements

The Publishers would like to thank the following for permission to reproduce photographs: AKG p. **47**; Auschwitz-Birkenau State Museum pp. **19**, **27**, **14**, **16**, **17**, **22**, **24**, **37**, **45**; Corbis p. **29**; Dr Roy Winkelman/Florida Centre for Instructional Technology p. **18**; Emma Robertson & Magnet Harlequin pp. **12**, **20** (top), **20** (bottom), **21** (top), **21** (bottom), **28**, **35**, **36** (1), **36** (2), **36** (3), **36** (4), **44** (top), **44** (bottom); Mary Evans Picture Library pp. **4**, **6**, **13**, **31**; Mauthausen Museum Archive pp. **25**, **39**, **46**; Mittel-Dora p. **33**; Ullstein Bilderdienst pp. **30**, **32**; USHMM pp. **10**, **11**, **15**, **23**, **26**, **38**, **40**, **41**; Wiener Library pp. **7**, **9**; Yad Vashem pp. **8**, **34**, **42**, **43**.

Cover photograph shows female prisoners at Auschwitz concentration camp just after liberation by the Soviet Army on 26 January 1945, reproduced with permission of USHMM.

The publishers would like to thank Jonathan Gorsky of the Council of Christians and Jews for his assistance in the preparation of this book.

Disclaimer

Contents

Words appearing in the text in bold, **like this**, are explained in the Glossary.

The camp system

In 1933 the **Nazi** Party, led by Adolf Hitler, came to power in Germany. The Nazis wanted to create a new German empire, the **Third Reich**. This empire was to be far bigger than Germany, so would have to take over other countries. The Nazis wanted the Third Reich to be full of Germans who would obey Hitler and the Nazis. They began to take action against anyone who might oppose them or who did not fit their idea of a German citizen.

Setting up the camp system

The Nazis began by arresting anyone they saw as a **political** opponent. They did not put these people in prison; instead they set up special prison camps. These camps were different from ordinary prisons because all the prisoners in the camps were imprisoned without trial and had no date for their release. They lived and worked in appalling conditions and they died, or were killed, in large numbers.

The camps were very effective. By 1935 there were very few people left in Germany who were willing to openly oppose the Nazis. However, the Nazis did not close the camps. Instead they started to fill them with various kinds of people whom they labelled '**undesirable**'. The camps played a large part in the **Holocaust** – the deliberate and systematic attempt by the Nazis to kill all **Jewish** people in Nazi-controlled lands. We cannot be sure how many people died in the Holocaust, but many historians agree that about 5.8 million were killed. Most of these died in the camps.

Three main types of camp developed: concentration camps, labour camps and death camps. They were run by the **SS** – a special military unit that swore loyalty to Hitler, rather than Germany. This book will try to show what life was like for prisoners in the camps.

Surviving the camps

Millions of people died in the camps, but some survived. The women and children here were liberated from Auschwitz camp after the war. They were especially lucky to survive. The Nazis saw women and children as less useful because they were not as strong as men. So the Nazis often killed the women and children straightaway.

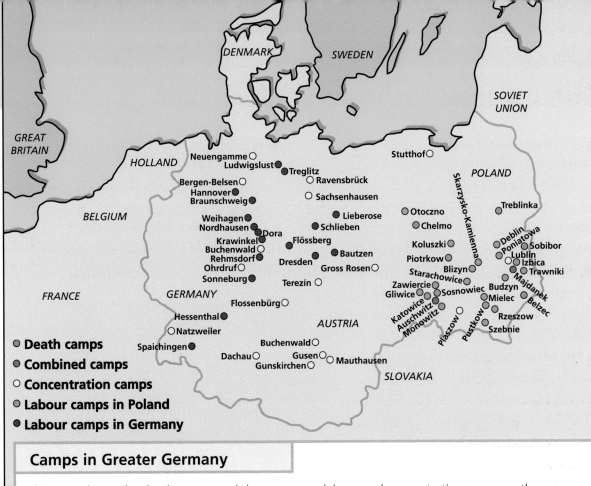

- ○ **Death camps**
- ● **Combined camps**
- ○ **Concentration camps**
- ○ **Labour camps in Poland**
- ● **Labour camps in Germany**

Camps in Greater Germany

This map shows the death camps and the biggest concentration camps and labour camps set up by the Nazis in **Greater Germany** (*see list on page 48*). It does not show the smaller labour and concentration camps or the many sub-camps that grew around the big camps. Nor does it show camps in other parts of German-**occupied** Europe.

How do we know?

- One of the most important sources of information comes from people who survived the camps. Camp prisoners are the only people who know exactly what life was like. Some told their memories directly – others wrote stories and poems or painted and drew the camps.
- Some who did not survive hid writings or pictures that were found later.
- There are official Nazi documents that show what went on in the camps. These only give the Nazi view of camp life. At the end of the war, the Nazis tried to destroy this evidence of what went on in the camps, but many records and photos have survived.
- A few camps still stand, such as Mauthausen and Auschwitz-Birkenau.
- After the war some Nazis, especially many who had been in the SS, were imprisoned and tried for war crimes. These trials heard evidence from survivors, members of the SS and people who worked for the SS in the camps.
- The soldiers who **liberated** the camps recorded what they were like in words, on film and in pictures.

5

The camps

There were several sorts of camps, and the system was expanded and changed over time. The people who were imprisoned changed and so did the **Nazis**' reasons for imprisoning them. Some things did not change. The camps were always run by the **SS**, short for '*Schutzstaffel*' – security staff, a special military unit that began as Hitler's special bodyguard. People were always sent to these camps without trial and for as long as the SS wanted them there. Conditions in the camps were always brutal.

Who was sent to the camps?

Between 1933 and 1935 **political** opponents of the Nazis were the most likely people to be sent to the camps. At first, the Nazis concentrated on **Communists**. The camps, and the laws allowing the police to send people to the camps without trial, were set up after the Reichstag (the German Parliament) was burnt down in 1933. The Nazis made it seem as if Communists started the fire. Very soon, however, the Nazis started arresting leaders and members of any other political parties or **trade unions** as 'political' opponents of the Nazi party.

Types of camp

- Concentration camps were the first Nazi camps. The Nazis said concentration camp prisoners would be 're-educated' to accept Nazi beliefs by 'exercise, discipline and hard work', and then released. Some were – many were not.

- The Nazis also set up labour camps, near factories or workplaces such as stone quarries, to provide cheap workers. Even in labour camps, work was never the chief point. The most important point was to work prisoners to death. As the war went on both the concentration camps and labour camps set up smaller sub-camps, near factories, quarries or mines.

- Death camps were set up, from 1941 on, to kill as many **Jews** as possible, as efficiently as possible. Four new camps were built as death camps: Chelmno, Belzec, Sobibor and Treblinka. Death camps were also added to two existing camps, Majdanek and Auschwitz.

No more camps?

By 1935, most political opposition to the Nazis was crushed or so secret that few opponents were caught. The Nazis considered closing the camps – there were just 3,000 prisoners left in them, the lowest number since they were first set up. But Hitler and the other Nazi leaders decided to expand the camps system, instead. They began to fill the camps with different kinds of people, all of whom the Nazis saw as '**undesirable**'.

Asocials

'**Asocials**' were people who the Nazis saw as failing in their duty to the state. This group included people who refused to work, drunks, gamblers, people who fell into debt and people who were seen as not bringing up their children properly. It also included homosexuals and people from groups that refused to swear an oath of loyalty to Hitler, such as **Jehovah's Witnesses**.

Transit camps

From 1938 onwards, Germany began to take control, usually by force, of other European countries. Jews and non-Aryans from these countries were sent to the camps. Transit camps, like this one in Drancy in France, were set up in **occupied** countries like France, Holland and Belgium. Millions of people were held in these camps until they could be taken to camps in Germany or Czechoslovakia and Poland – countries under German control.

Racial inferiors

The Nazis had complicated, entirely invented ideas about **race**. The Nazis wanted to fill the **Third Reich** with 'pure' Germans, who they saw as belonging to an invented race called **Aryans**. The other western European groups were beneath the Aryans. More inferior were western European peoples, Asian peoples, then Slavs, Gypsies and, worst of all to the Nazis, Jews.

Running the camps

The SS ran the camps. Although they were a military unit, they reported directly to the SS commander, Heinrich Himmler. Himmler reported directly to Hitler. Each camp, however small, had a camp **commandant** and some guards. In between came a varying number of SS officers who organized supplies and equipment as well as other aspects of camp life – hiring prisoners out as workers, for example.

Kapos

The camps were organized so that some prisoners, called **kapos**, did the actual day-to-day supervision of other prisoners. *Kapos* were mostly chosen from criminals, preferably German criminals.

Kapos reported to the SS and were given privileges for working for the SS. So *kapos* in charge of work groups did not have to do any of the hard, difficult work themselves. *Kapos* had the power to punish, even murder, other prisoners. But they were, like all the other prisoners, entirely at the mercy of the SS and could lose their job at any time. Ana Novac remembers the *blockälteste* in charge of her barracks:

> 'Felicie is in charge of our barracks. Her "place in the sun" gets her quite a bit of extra bread and jam, but makes her very tense, nervous. She arrives two hours before each **roll call**, counts and recounts us 25 times and yet she still gets it wrong. So the Germans slap her, in front of us, and she slaps us, in return.'

Meeting at roll call

The camp commandant met with some of his officers, and looked over the prisoners, at roll call each day. In this photo, the camp commandant (with his back to us) is being given the daily report on the number of prisoners who had died that day.

Female *kapos*

The women's camps had female *kapos*. They dressed like the other prisoners, although their clothes were usually more suited to the weather – they had coats in winter, for example. In this picture of the weaving shed at Ravensbrück camp, in Germany, the women with headscarves are ordinary prisoners. The woman on the left of the aisle with a long dark coat and a cap is probably a *kapo*.

Constant fear

The SS did not want revolts or escape attempts in the camps. So they worked hard to stop prisoners making friends and meeting in groups. They promised extra rations or better work to people who informed on other prisoners. They made punishments very harsh to increase the atmosphere of fear and terror. Prisoners could be hung for a minor offence, like meeting in a group. The SS changed work gangs around and moved people from camp to camp. All of this, added to the hundreds of deaths every day, made it hard for prisoners to form trustworthy groups.

Different camp experiences

A prisoner's camp life varied depending on various factors.

- The year: In the early 1930s, when the camps were mainly used to imprison political opponents, it was possible to be released from them. Even Jewish prisoners were released. Many of them were convinced by their camp experiences and left Germany.
- The camp: The sort of camp people were sent to was important. Small labour camps could be less brutal than bigger camps, such as Auschwitz. Death camps were different – people, mostly Jews, were sent there to be killed.
- The guards: What life was like also depended on who was in charge of your daily routine. Some guards were more brutal than others.
- The prisoners: A prisoner's race affected their camp experience. German criminals, who the SS used as *kapos*, had a very different life from Jewish prisoners, who were the least important.

Processing arrivals

As soon as they arrived in the camps, prisoners were not seen as people any longer. They went through a step-by-step process intended to strip away the things that made them human individuals. Even though many of them had already been in prison and badly treated by the **Gestapo**, the **Nazi** police, most new prisoners were not prepared for the indignity of arriving at their first camp.

The same system

In almost all camps the arrival process was the same for new prisoners and for prisoners being transferred from other camps.

- Prisoners were made to undress.
- All the prisoners' hair was shaved.
- Prisoners had to shower.
- They were given uniforms and a camp number.
- Finally, the prisoners were herded off to barracks. All new prisoners, and some who were moved from other camps, then spent several days in '**quarantine**' – cut off from the rest of the camp until they 'learned' camp routine.

Mieczyslaw Karczewski remembers arriving at Mauthausen:

'The first shock was when this **SS** guy comes up and he says, take off your clothes. I thought, where? You mean here? It was raining; we were weak from a long **transport**, hungry, too. They had made us stand for hours at some wall and now they were expecting us to take our clothes off. We stood there naked in the snow and rain ... Then we were given a number and off to the barracks.'

Dogs

New arrivals in Mauthausen camp were met by SS guards with dogs trained to attack prisoners. Leon Zelman, a **political** prisoner who survived the camp, remembers that the dogs were used to terrorize prisoners on a daily basis:

'The SS men and their dogs were behind us every day as we came back from work. If anyone collapsed they were there right away, the dogs attacking and barking ferociously. Anyone who did not get back on their feet after this was shot in the neck.'

Arriving in Mauthausen

Arrivals at Mauthausen were processed in the large central square. This was also used for **roll call** and disinfection – large scale hosing down with chemicals to kill **lice**.

Fear and uncertainty

Whilst the process of dealing with new arrivals was usually the same, the SS made sure that there were enough differences to keep the prisoners terrified and uncertain. Sometimes, they unloaded trains or trucks at once and made the new arrivals rush through the processing routine 'at the double' – running. At other times, they made the process last all day, with the prisoners standing around, often naked, in snow, rain or baking heat. Survivors remember the fear and uncertainty at every stage and the certainty that the SS would beat people to death or shoot them for any reason, real or imagined.

Less than human

The camp system tried to take away prisoners' individuality during the arrivals process. From then on, the system was designed to continue to treat people as if they were less than human to underline how little their lives were worth.

Tadeusz Sobolewicz remembers arriving at Auschwitz camp, aged seventeen, puzzled by the brutality of the SS, and even more so by that of the **kapos**:

> 'All the time I was asking myself: "why are they beating us so? Why?" The kapos were prisoners like us yet they beat us so eagerly, as if we were their enemies ... Why didn't anyone explain what we should do, instead of hitting us first?'

The SS and the kapos used prisoners' camp numbers, not their name. Prisoners worked and lived as part of a barrack or work group – not as individuals. When the arrivals process was over, it was hard for family and friends to recognize each other – everyone looked the same. This made it easier for the SS to control and mistreat prisoners, because they did not see them as people.

The purpose of quarantine

New arrivals were sent to quarantine. This was supposed to be a medical quarantine, to make sure the new arrivals did not have any diseases that could spread to the rest of the camp. In fact, quarantine was to terrorize the new arrivals so that, when they joined the rest of the camp, they would be obedient and work hard. Roman Frister, a Polish **Jew** who survived four different camps, said: 'The Nazis surrounded us not only with barbed wire, but also with a wall of orders and rules that demanded blind obedience.'

Quarantine barracks

This is a photograph of the quarantine barracks in Auschwitz-Birkenau camp. They looked just like the other barracks, but were separated by a fence. The quarantine prisoners were not allowed to mix with other prisoners.

Herr Kahn was arrested in 1938 and sent to Buchenwald camp, where he and the rest of the men arrested at the same time spent two days and three nights in quarantine:

'There were about 6000 of us crowded into one barracks which didn't have a floor yet, it was just damp clay. We had bare planks for beds, no mattresses, no blankets, no light. The toilets were disgusting. In the middle of the first night, when things had quietened down a little, we were suddenly blinded by flashlights and about a dozen men were dragged away by the SS. We heard them screaming horribly outside and they never came back. The same thing happened the next two nights. On the third morning we were lined up in front of the barracks ... Everyone with a visible injury was asked how it happened. The first few answered truthfully, saying the SS had whipped them. The guards then whipped them over and over until they said they had done it themselves. Then we were led away to new barracks, where conditions were a little better.'

Waiting for death

A group of Jewish people transported to Auschwitz-Birkenau death camp from Hungary. The SS photographed them as they waited to be gassed. The SS had told them that they would have a shower and move on to be resettled the next day.

Arriving in Treblinka

Treblinka was a death camp. Prisoners sent to Treblinka were gassed as soon as possible after their arrival, usually within two hours. A hundred or so *Arbeitsjuden*, 'work **Jews**', were kept alive to keep the camp running – maintaining the SS barracks, processing the possessions of the new arrivals and disposing of the bodies of the dead.

Willi Mentz was an SS man who worked in Treblinka. His job was to shoot the sick and frail from the transports. They were taken off to the so-called hospital area, where they were shot. Presumably it reassured the prisoners if they thought the sick were getting special care.

Mentz described the arrival and processing at Treblinka:

'When the Jews got out of the wagons they were told they were a **resettlement** transport, that they would be given a shower and new clothes and taken on to where they would live the next day. The women undressed in huts, the men out in the open. The women and children were led down a passageway called "the tube" to the **gas chambers** ... There were always ill and frail people on the wagons, as well as dead people. The bodies were unloaded and the sick and frail were brought to the hospital. They were collected up by an open grave and I shot them in the neck. Sometimes there were only two or three, sometimes twenty or more – men, women and children.'

Friends and societies

The **SS** tried hard to stop prisoners in the camp setting up any kinds of groups or even making friends. This was because societies, such as groups of people with the same religious beliefs, could help each other. Groups could plot revolts or escapes, and friends helped to keep each other going.

Breaking up families

The first thing the SS did was to break up family groups. They divided up the camps by sexes – women and young children in one place, men and older boys in another. Family members did still try to stay together, and some managed it. At the age of seventeen, Hugo Gryn was sent to Auschwitz with his father and uncle. They managed to stay together through changes of camp, but they did not all survive the brutal conditions. Hugo's uncle died in Lieberose camp. His father died in Gunskirchen camp a few days after the **Allies** reached the camp at the end of the war, in 1945.

Selection at Auschwitz

Selections were often made as soon as a train arrived at Auschwitz. The SS sent the old, the young, the sick and many of the women to the left, and healthy men and boys and some of the women to the right. This photo shows women and children who were sent to their death at Auschwitz-Birkenau camp.

Eli Wiesel remembers how his family was divided:

'An SS officer came to meet us, a truncheon in his hand. He gave the order: "Men to the left! Women to the right!" Eight words spoken quietly, without emotion. Eight sort, simple words. Yet that was the moment when I parted from my mother. I had not had time to think, but already I felt the pressure of my father's hand: we were alone. For a part of a second I glimpsed my mother and my sisters moving away to the right. Tzipora held Mother's hand. I saw them disappear into the distance; my mother was stroking my sister's fair hair, as though to protect her, while I walked on with my father and the other men.'

14

Sisters who survived

These two Italian sisters were **political** prisoners imprisoned in Gusen camp, in Germany. They both survived the camps. This photo was taken when the camp was liberated.

Family support

Whole families could not stay together, but if those of the same sex could do so, it helped them to keep going. They had emotional support and a practical advantage. They could deal with camp life as a team – they could trust each other. This was much harder for strangers meeting for the first time.

Ana Novac, who was alone when she arrived in Plaszow camp, remembers the three Falk sisters:

'Each one had her job. Ruchi, the oldest and strongest, was the boss. Feigele's job was to show her dimples, act innocent, try to charm extra food or a soft job out of the **kapos**. Surele did whatever else was needed. She was a weak and growing child if there was something left at the bottom of the soup pot. She was sick if she didn't want to work in bad weather. She was strong as an ox if there was a paid job going. Needless to say they managed to get the job of giving out the food for the barrack.'

Gerda Weissmann, a seventeen-year-old Polish girl, and her sister, Ilse, were sent from Bielitz to Bolkenhain camp in June 1942. They managed to stay together through six changes of camp, all of them small sub-camps, but Ilse died on the 'death march' into Germany ahead of the advancing Allied armies: '"Promise me one thing," she said. "You must try to keep going for one more week." I did not answer. "One more week, promise," she persisted. "I promise."' Gerda kept her promise. On the fourth day she was **liberated**.

Making friends

Many people formed friendships on the **transports** and in the camps. And some people came across friends from their old life in the camps. Ana Novac met an old friend in Auschwitz-Birkenau:

> 'I was suddenly lifted off my feet, hugged and there was my old friend Edith, beaming at me. She was a camp cook. She took off her uniform dress (she was wearing another one under it) and I put it on, there, out in the open. She then ran off and came back with a steaming bowl – meat and potatoes all from the bottom of the soup pot.'

Keeping friends

Friendships made things easier – but could be broken up by the SS moving people around, or by death. Also, the camps affected different people in different ways – they could change your friends dramatically.

Fania Fenelon, a French singer, met a woman called Clara on the train from Drancy transit camp in France to Auschwitz. They shared their food and promised to stick together. When Fania was chosen for the camp orchestra, she refused to stay without Clara. Being in the orchestra gave them much better living conditions than the ordinary prisoners.

But Clara found even this hard to cope with. She refused to share food, then began to suspect the others of taking her food. She cut herself off from them. Then Clara was made a *kapo*:

> 'She stood in front of our little group and pushed her club under our noses. "From now on, I'm the boss. I'm in charge and you do as I say or I'll hit you!" Drunk with noise and violence she lashed out at the weakest and strutted about, claiming to the SS that her block was the most efficient.'

Musical society

Fania Fenelon was in the women's orchestra at Auschwitz-Birkenau. Several camps had orchestras. The orchestras played marching tunes as prisoners went to and from work each day. They also played concerts for the SS. They were, unusually, a society set up by the SS. This photo, taken by the SS, shows the men's orchestra at Auschwitz I.

Taking chances

There were people in the camp who took the chance to help anyone they could, as this picture drawn by a survivor shows.

People who worked in the kitchens sometimes managed to smuggle some extra food out. They often got this food to the hospital. Patients in the hospital were given what the SS called 'lazy' rations – less food because they were not working. So they had less nourishment just when they needed it most. A bowl of soup, even camp soup, could make all the difference.

Keeping to themselves

There were times when even your closest friends could not help you. Lucie Adelsberger, a **Jewish** doctor in Auschwitz, remembers that it was a rule among the prisoners, as well as an official SS rule, that you did not act to help a friend or family member who was being mistreated. It never helped. Neither the SS nor the *kapos* would listen to a prisoner asking them to spare another prisoner. Lucie Adelsberger remembers one such incident:

'During **roll call** the whole block had to kneel in the snow because the prisoners who worked in the weaving mill had failed, by only a few metres, to make enough cloth in the day. A girl, weak with fever, fell over and the *kapos* began beating her. The girl's mother protested. The *kapos* responded by kicking and beating the daughter even harder and they beat up the mother as well, for her protests.'

Horrors like this made many people decide that the best way to survive was not to have any friends. They found it easier to cut off their emotions entirely. They concentrated on keeping themselves alive.

Other supports

Some people learned to cope with life in the camp by hating the SS and wanting to defeat them by surviving. Others were kept going by a sense of humour or determination to survive. There were also organized activities, which kept people going. Some were secret from the **Nazis**, others were not.

Prisoners organized football matches and other entertainments on Sunday afternoons. Sometimes these were organized by *kapos*. One *kapo* at Mauthausen, Franz Unek, even had wooden cups made to present to the winning team. Stanislaw Gorondowski, a prisoner in Mauthausen, remembers:

> 'There were football games, boxing matches, drama and circus shows organized by the prisoners. And one must not forget the orchestras. All this was a huge contrast to SS brutality, yet they let it happen, they seemed somehow impressed by these shows.'

Music

Some camps had orchestras. The SS had to approve before an orchestra could be set up. In several camps, including Auschwitz, the SS set up the orchestra. There were several reasons for this. One was to provide marching music to get everyone to and from work. Another was to show the outside world that camps were not so bad. Even new arrivals were encouraged and asked themselves: 'How bad could a camp be, if there was an orchestra there?' Finally, the SS could order a camp orchestra to give concerts of the SS's favourite music at any time.

The French singer Fania Fenelon remembers that she was grateful for being in the orchestra, because it kept her alive. But she also felt angry at having to play for the SS and guilty when she played to the other prisoners and saw how much worse their conditions were.

For the children

The women of Auschwitz-Birkenau's women's camp decorated the walls of this barrack. They painted pictures from traditional fairy stories for the children who lived there.

Secret radios

Some factory workers stole parts to make secret radios like this one. They could then listen to the news and to religious services on the radio.

Religious beliefs

Many camp prisoners were comforted by their religious beliefs. Religious services were banned, but people did manage to hold services sometimes. For example, on Sunday, 16 November 1941, Konrad Szweda, a Catholic priest, held a mass secretly in Block 4 in Auschwitz I camp. The mass was as short as possible and held in a dark, cramped aisle between the bunk beds. If they had been caught, everyone at the mass would have been executed.

Hugo Gryn, who was sent to his first camp at just seventeen, and his fellow **Jews** in Block 4 in Lieberose camp decided to celebrate the Jewish festival of Hanukkah, which fell in the first week of December in 1944. They decided to light a **menorah** every night.

They made the *menorah* with pieces of metal and wood. They saved their margarine to make candles, with wicks made from twisted threads from the edges of their caps. Finally, the first night of Hanukkah arrived and they met to light the *menorah*. Several Catholics and Protestants, even the *blockälteste* himself, came too. They chanted the prayers. Hugo, the youngest there, tried to light the candles. They would not light because margarine does not burn. Hugo complained to his father about the waste of the margarine. He remembers his father's reply:

'Patiently he taught me one of the most lasting lessons of my life and I believe that he made my survival possible. "Don't be so angry," he said to me, "you know that this festival celebrates the victory of the spirit over tyranny and might. You and I have had to go once for over a week without proper food and another time almost three days without water, but you cannot live for three minutes without hope."'

Living conditions

Living conditions varied from camp to camp. In the bigger camps, conditions were often harder – there was less space, the food was worse, the discipline was harsher. Conditions were never good anywhere, but there were camps where the conditions were bearable. When Ana Novac, a young Hungarian girl, was in Auschwitz-Birkenau she shared a single sleeping space with four other women. When she was transferred to a small work camp at Wiesau she was amazed by the difference:

> 'We are told we will wash daily, that there will be hot water to wash in. There are four or five rooms to each barrack, twenty bunks to a room and one person to a bunk. One! With a blanket! A pillow! A spoon and a real plate! The soup is real, proper soup, too, and the bread is fresh.'

These conditions were unusually good.

Housing

In most camps the prisoners lived in barracks. Where there was overcrowding, or where the prisoners were building a new camp, they lived in tents. Wherever they were, the prisoners were crowded together. They either slept on the floor – if they were lucky they got straw or straw mattresses to sleep on, or in bunks. If they slept in bunks, it was usually several prisoners to a bunk. In these conditions diseases, **lice** and fleas spread rapidly. Ana Novac remembers conditions in Auschwitz-Birkenau:

Sleeping places

These photos show the bunks in Auschwitz I and the sleeping shelves in Auschwitz-Birkenau. People usually slept three or four to a bunk, with straw mattresses. The sleeping shelves usually had eight to ten people in them.

> 'They say a **transport** of Italian women are to be moved into our barrack. They turn out to be Greeks, from Rhodes. What difference, anyway? It is 300 more to argue over blankets and space. Now you can only all turn over together ... It's impossible to sleep on your back – even raising my knees a little causes grumbling from all sides.'

Sanitation

Camp barracks, toilets and washrooms were painted with sayings like: 'Cleanliness is your duty'. Despite this, camp **sanitation** was so bad that it was impossible for prisoners to keep clean. Prisoners often had to cope using a few wells or a tap or two outside for washing and a huge toilet pit. Even with toilets and washrooms prisoners were not allowed to use them sensibly. They had a minute or so to wash in the mornings and a similar amount of time to use the toilets. They were not allowed to leave the barracks at night. Sometimes they were given a toilet bucket to use, sometimes not.

Disinfection

The **SS** regularly disinfected prisoners. They made this as unpleasant as possible – prisoners had to wait while naked. Sometimes they had to run around the nearest square, or do exercises. Some prisoners died during each disinfection. Tadeusz Sobolewicz remembers:

'It took three hours for us to get to the vat. We had been naked all the time ... When we got there they were dragging a body out of the tub. There were already four corpses stacked against the wall. I quickly climbed into the tub. The water was freezing, but it also burned me – there was clearly too much chlorine in the tub. But I went right under – before they could push me under and hold me there.'

Washrooms and toilets

These photos show the washroom and toilets in Auschwitz I. When the camps were in use they would have been full of people desperate to use them. Prisoners were only allowed into them for a short time first thing in the morning.

Three meals a day

Camp prisoners were given three meals a day: breakfast, a meal some time after noon and one in the evening. The SS set down rules for what these meals were to be.

The menus were based on providing the least amount of food to keep people alive and working – so non-working prisoners, such as those in hospital, were given less. The average ration for a worker, in most camps was: 500ml of coffee or tea for breakfast. Dinner was 750 ml of soup, with meat four times a week. The evening meal was 300g of bread, 25g of margarine, 25g of sausage or cheese and a teaspoonful of jam. Prisoners seldom got even this.

Desperate for food

This picture was painted by a camp prisoner after the camps had been **liberated**. It shows how the prisoners were so desperate for food that they would scoop up even the disgusting 'camp soup' from the ground to eat it.

The quality of food

The food provided was tested from time to time, by the SS Hygienic Institute that created the menus in the first place. A report carried out by Dr Hans Munch noted that the soup served in Auschwitz I was regularly missing well over half the fat it should have had. The prisoners' sausage had half the fat of the sausage eaten by the SS, despite the fact that they were both made in the same place and were supposed to be made to the same recipe. Coffee and tea were made from ground up acorns or birch leaves. The soup, bread and jam often included sawdust and other, less edible things, like sand or pebbles.

Food parcels

The camp rules said that prisoners could be sent food parcels. In 1943 the **Red Cross** began to send parcels, too. These parcels had to be addressed to people by name, giving the camp name and the prisoner's camp number. It was hard for the Red Cross to get this information – so many parcels were sent straight to the SS canteen or the camp kitchens. Even properly addressed parcels did not always make it to the prisoner they were sent to.

Parcels were checked by the SS (for weapons and so on, supposedly) and while checking, they took whatever they wanted. In 1944 all camp **commandants** were told that all parcels from outside **Greater Germany**, from people or organizations, were to be sent to the camp kitchens, even if they were properly addressed.

Too weak to eat

Constant underfeeding left many prisoners too weak to eat when they were liberated. These prisoners at Ebensee camp have been given sugar cubes to suck to keep their strength up.

'Cooking with the mouth'

In all the camps, big or small, people were starving. Yet many prisoners, men and women, talked about food. Some even wrote recipes down. Gerda Weissmann, who was first sent to the camps as a teenager, remembers:

'In Helmbrechts, a small camp of perhaps a dozen barracks, we were all sick. We had very little food, because we were not working anymore … many of the girls began talking about food. They started to swap recipes for the richest pastries and cakes they could think of. I found it terrible to listen to, it made my hunger worse.'

Susan E. Cernyak-Spatz, who had been a prisoner in Auschwitz and Terezín, says:

'There was a camp expression for all the talk of food. We called it "cooking with the mouth". Everybody did it. And people got very upset if they thought you made a dish the wrong way, or used the wrong ingredients.'

Illness

Everyone got sick in the camps. The crowded conditions, dreadful sanitation and poor food meant that diseases, especially dysentery and typhus, spread quickly and hit almost everyone. **TB** and other lung diseases also spread quickly. Prisoners soon realized that they had to hide their sickness as long as they could. There were several reasons for this.

Less food

Often those in hospital were put on 'lazy' rations – smaller portions of food – because they were not working. Even if food was sent to the hospital, the patients did not often get to eat it. Patients who were sent to act as nurses often kept the food for themselves. Even when they gave food to the patients, many were too sick to eat it or too weak to feed themselves.

Inadequate treatment

The sick did not get proper medical treatment in hospital. They were dumped there to get better by themselves or die. Some camps allowed prisoners who were doctors to work in the hospitals and give the prisoners some care. They very seldom gave them any medicines for the patients, though. In other camps, doctors and other patients had to look after the sick secretly. Doctors, while not expected to care for the sick, were expected to fill out detailed forms on each patient every day. They also had to make sure that they had the right number of patients there – otherwise they would be beaten.

Experiments

These are some of the drugs that the SS tested on prisoners for the firm I.G. Farben. The drugs often had horrific side effects and were not made for general use. The sick in the hospitals were guinea pigs for these drugs. Drug testing only went on in the larger camps, where SS doctors had many **Jewish** people on hand to use in their experiments. The prisoners experimented on were mainly Jewish, because the Nazis saw them as the most worthless.

'Raspberry picking'

In Mauthausen the sick were often given a tin cup and told that they were going to do 'light work' picking berries. While being marched along, they were shot by the SS – supposedly while 'trying to escape', like the prisoner shown here. The SS liked these 'raspberry picking details' because guards who shot prisoners trying to escape were often given time off in reward.

No value

The sick could not work. So the SS saw them as a drain on the camp. This is why they did not provide the hospitals with anything they needed to care for the sick. Erwin Gostner, a prisoner who survived Mauthausen, remembers:

> 'The sick lie on straw bags and are left there, with no care, until they are dead. Then they are stacked up in the washroom for the daily collection ... New patients are stacked straight on to the straw bags the dead have left, which are smeared with blood and filth.'

Killed off

If the sick did not die quickly enough, they were 'helped'. In Mauthausen this 'help' included long **roll calls** outside in their underwear or cold showers out in the open. The SS also held **selections** of the sickest almost daily – the selected prisoners were killed at once. The selections were made by SS doctors. The selected patients were killed in various ways. They could just be left without food or water, to starve. But this was slow and did not free a bed for the next sick person. So the SS hurried their deaths along. The doctors might kill them by injecting a drug, usually phenol, which gave them a heart attack. Otherwise, the SS gassed or shot them.

Discipline

The camps had a strict set of rules and a harsh system of punishments. These were worked out for Dachau camp, the first camp set up. They were later applied to all camps. While the official rules and punishments were hard, camp life was harder. In reality, the SS could punish prisoners for anything or nothing and could make up any punishments they wanted. **Kapos** and other prisoner-functionaries were encouraged to make up cruel punishments, especially for Jewish prisoners.

Learning the rules

Often, prisoners were not told the rules; they had to work them out for themselves. This added to the atmosphere of fear and uncertainty in the camp.

A beating

This photo shows an SS guard beating a prisoner at Poniatowa camp, in Poland. Beatings took place every day.

Ana Novac remembers one incident in Auschwitz-Birkenau:

'We had a shock this morning. The new arrivals have cut up several blankets to wrap around themselves! "It's cold," they explain to Solange, the speechless *kapo*. So now they have to stay on their knees during roll call for the next four days and have no food at all for two. At roll call the SS in charge, whips them without mercy.'

Punishments

Groups of prisoners were often punished by day-long roll calls. At these roll calls prisoners had to stand to attention, to remove and replace their caps and do various other things all day. The prisoners had no food or drink. If they did anything wrong, they were beaten, sometimes to death. Some died from exhaustion. Individual prisoners could be punished by beatings or whipping. They could be hung from beams or made to kneel on piles of sharp stones for hours. They could be sent to the camp prison to be locked in the cells or sent to the punishment unit – a special barrack where they had to work harder for longer and were given less food. Prisoners sent to the punishment unit were not expected to survive.

Missing roll call

It was serious for the SS when a prisoner was not at roll call. Perhaps the prisoner had escaped? Camp rules did not say that missing roll call was punishable by death, but in many camps this was what happened. Sometimes prisoners were sent to the punishment unit, which worked prisoners to death. At other times they were simply beaten to death in front of the other prisoners. Ana Novac remembers this in Plaszow camp:

'The count was off. There was one missing. They counted over and over. She was found in the barracks, asleep. She was taken out to the roll call square … It went dead quiet, as if everyone there had stopped breathing all at once. We knew she was lost.

'She hadn't realized yet, she was new … He ordered her to undress, then carefully took off his leather jacket and folded it, putting it on the ground well out of the way. This careful preparation for murder upset me more than what followed. He beat her to death. Luckily, she fainted almost at once.'

Roll call

This painting of roll call in Auschwitz I on a Christmas Eve was painted by a camp prisoner after the camps were liberated and the war was over. You can see a *kapo* hitting a prisoner and an SS officer adding up the counts in his book. You can also see the pile of people who have already died at this roll call. In the block of prisoners on the left at the front of the picture you can see another person who has died and has not yet been moved to the pile.

Work

Every prisoner in every kind of camp had to work, unless they were sick. Because the sick were simply sent to the hospital to die, people worked on for as long as they could. Eventually, the prisoners became a vital part of **Nazi** war production. More and more often, camps and sub-camps were built with factories or near existing factories.

However, work had another purpose. The camps were expected to work people to death. This was the Nazi idea of *Vernichtung durch Arbeit*: destruction through work. From the start, work of all kinds, in all camps, was expected to kill all but the strongest within months or even weeks. Every job was made as difficult and dangerous as possible. Had the Nazis wanted their prisoners working efficiently they would have provided basic tools, such as wheelbarrows for shifting heavy loads.

Arbeit Macht Frei

These are the gates of Auschwitz I. Several camp gates had *Arbeit Macht Frei* on them: 'Work will set you Free'. This sounds as if the Nazis were saying: 'If you work hard and learn your lesson, you will be allowed to go home.' This was not the message at all – work only set Nazi prisoners free by killing them. Karl Fritzsch, *Schutzhaftlagerfürher* (camp **commandant**) at Auschwitz I, made the same speech to all prisoners when they arrived, telling them what to expect:

> 'This is not a sanatorium but a German concentration camp. There is only one exit: through the **crematorium** chimney. **Jews** may live for two weeks, priests for one month, the rest for three months. Anyone who does not like what I say can throw himself on the electric fence. That, too, is a way out.'

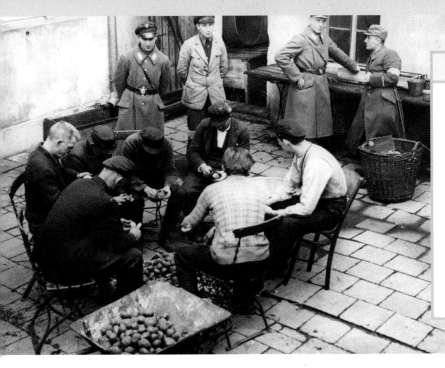

Building the camps

The first camp prisoners often had to build the camp. They lived in tents, or old buildings already on the site, until they built the barracks. Once the camps were built, prisoners kept them running. They worked in the kitchens, offices, hospitals and stores. They cleaned the camp, dug ditches and built additions to the camp.

Depending on where the camp was built, the prisoners were also sent to work in nearby factories, mines, steelworks or quarries. The **SS**, who ran the camps, made a profit from hiring out their prisoners.

Different kinds of work

Different prisoners did different work – the SS made clear distinctions among them. Criminals, especially German criminals, got the easy jobs and could become **kapos** – put in charge of other prisoners. Jews and other groups seen by the Nazis as racially inferior got the worst jobs. Tadeusz Sobolewicz, a Polish **political** prisoner, remembers:

> 'We had to unload sacks of cement. They were heavy, but manageable. But the **SS** made us move them running, "at the double", beaten for every act of "sabotage", such as letting a sack fall.'

Dangerous games

The SS could turn almost any job into a dangerous game. Kitchen work was seen as a good job, but every day about 20 prisoners died while moving boxes of potatoes to the kitchens at Auschwitz I. They died because the SS made their job impossible.

Two prisoners carried each box, which weighed more than two fit men could carry. If they fell, the box crushed them, or they were clubbed to death for dropping it. If they kept on their feet they were still likely to drop the box and be killed for doing so.

Skilled workers?

Camp prisoners soon saw that it was important to keep working. Working, especially in factories or other places that paid the SS, made them useful, so more likely to live. Factories preferred workers with useful skills. So when the SS asked at **roll call** for carpenters, lathe operators or cloth makers prisoners volunteered, even if they did not have these skills. Hugo Gryn told the SS he was a carpenter. At Lieberose camp, Hugo was told to:

> '"Oil those saws and then start cutting wood for tables and chairs. The designs and measurements are on that sheet." The oiling part was easy. I was made for oiling saws, I thought. But the chairs and tables – how was I going to cut those to measure? Just then an SS man came in and demanded wood for the guard room.'

Hugo cut some wood. The SS man did not tell him to stop, so he cut all the rest – a week's worth of wood. Luckily the *kapo* thought it was funny, and taught Hugo to do the job properly.

Women's work

Women prisoners were worked to death, too, and treated just as badly as the men. Magda Somogyi worked on road building in 1944:

> 'Once I dropped a huge stone because it was so heavy. The SS man whipped me for dropping the stone. From then on, every day he whipped me before work began saying: "Do you understand? You will learn that you do not need to drop the stone." He was right. I didn't drop a stone again.'

Other work that women had to do included digging drainage ditches knee-deep in swamp water and digging out the cesspits the block toilets drained into.

Ravensbrück

This is a picture of Ravensbrück camp. Ravensbrück was a women's camp – although men and women were locked in the prison. These were local 'politicals' who were kept there until the Nazis could decide which camp to send them to, or whether to execute them there.

More workers needed

At first, almost all prisoners were 'expendable' – not important enough to keep alive. As more Germans joined the armed forces, the Nazis ran short of workers to do vital war work. On 15 May 1943 all camp commandants were told:

> 'The urgency of the work being carried out by prisoners requires that every prisoner work to the highest level. Results must be improved by leading and educating the prisoners and by granting them privileges.'

Privileges included not standing for hours on roll call or not being beaten 'unnecessarily'. Prisoners could 'earn' extra food or tobacco. Privileges were given to prisoners doing the most 'technical' jobs. The hardest, most dangerous, work had no privileges.

A conflict of interests

The SS, who were responsible for organizing the work of the camps, understood the need for improved living and working conditions for the prisoners who did war work. The SS who ran individual camps often did not; many clung to the idea of 'death through work'. Both groups seemed to agree, however, that Jews were still to be brutally treated, rather than given improved conditions. In Mauthausen camp, for example, the death rate for most prisoners went down once they began doing war work. The death rate for Jews was close to 100 per cent all the time.

Mauthausen

On 8 August 1938, prisoners from Dachau camp were sent to the stone quarries of Wiener Graben, near Linz. They built Mauthausen camp, from stone, with their bare hands and very few tools. At first, the prisoners worked mainly in the quarries. Working hours were from 6.30 a.m. to 6.30 p.m. in the lightest part of the summer. Winter working hours were shorter, but the weather made conditions harder. The prisoners were often working barefoot in ice and snow. Milos Vitek, a Czech survivor from Mauthausen, remembers that just getting to work was an ordeal:

'As we went down the stairs to the quarry the *Blockführer* began to whip the last five in line. They tried to dodge the blows, so bumped into those in front. So the whole hundred-man unit fell in a tangle to the quarry at the bottom. Because we were not in a line the *kapos* then beat us with clubs. At this point we usually lost our wooden clogs, so had to do a day's work barefooted. There were several dead before the day's work even began.'

Digging stone

Work in the quarries, as shown here, continued all through the war. From the spring of 1943 the SS also began to make machine guns, aircraft engines and whole aircraft at Mauthausen. Prisoners built a set of sub-camps, including armament plants, some of which were underground. From December 1943 to December 1944 skilled workers were given bonus coupons that could be exchanged for food if there was any, at the canteen. Jews and other so-called racially inferior groups continued to work in the quarries. Their conditions did not improve.

A drawing of Dora, done after the war by Maurice de la Pintiere, a French prisoner there. Yves Beon, another prisoner, described his first view of the camp:

'The air was thick with dust, burnt oil fumes and humidity. Here are hills of gravel, there valleys filled with water. Grey creatures shovel, hollow out and tear away at surfaces. Narrow hoppers, loaded with stones and trash roll through the narrow passage, pushed by men in filthy rags … Others push, pull and drag insanely heavy loads. The SS, *kapos* and others move among them, shouting and swearing, whipping and clubbing the terrified prisoners. The sound of mine blasting adds to the noise and chaos.'

Building Dora

On 28 August 1943, 107 prisoners were taken in trucks from Buchenwald concentration camp to an old mine used as a petrol store by the Nazis. They were to be the first of thousands of prisoners working in a secret factory making a new German 'wonder weapon' – V-2 long-range rocket. The camp was named Dora. The prisoners first had to finish the underground factory. Their barracks were left until last. They slept on straw in the tunnels they were digging. There were no toilets or drains. The tunnels got very little air. They stank of sewage and poisonous gas from the explosives used to clear the tunnels.

In the first six months, 6000 prisoners died or were killed because they were too ill to work from the conditions.

Building rockets

By April 1944 Dora was ready. Conditions for the workers improved as they dug and moved into their own barracks. Also, because they were working on war production, the SS rules about improved conditions applied to them. This did not last. From November 1944 to April 1945, when the camp was **liberated**, more and more prisoners were marched to Dora from other camps ahead of the Russian army and conditions worsened.

Death in the camps

People died in all the **Nazi** camps, all the time. From the start the death rate was highest for prisoners the Nazis saw as racially inferior – Poles, Russians and especially **Jews**. Hitler had a fierce hatred for Jewish people, which he encouraged everyone in Germany, and the lands taken over by Germany, to share. He wanted to make these places *Judenfrei* – 'Jew Free'.

At first, the Nazis had tried to make life so difficult for Jewish people that they would leave Germany. But not enough left. Then the Nazis began to herd Jews into the camps, encouraging the **SS** to treat them so badly that they died. As the German army invaded Russia, death squads, called *Einsatzgruppen*, followed. Their job was to kill as many Jews as they could find. Even this did not get rid of the Jews quickly enough for Hitler.

The 'Final Solution'

On 20 January 1942, fifteen important Nazi leaders met in Wannsee, near Berlin, to agree on a 'Final Solution' to what the Nazis called the 'Jewish Problem'. Hitler was not there, but Reinhard Heydrich, who led the meeting and was put in charge of making its decisions work, made it clear the orders came from Hitler.

The conference decided that all Jews in lands controlled by Germany were to be killed. It was the job of the SS to find the most efficient way of doing this. This meant killing large numbers of people at once, quickly and cheaply. It also meant finding a way of killing that was not 'upsetting' for the SS men who did it.

Einsatzgruppen

The *Einsatzgruppen* shot Russian Jews, one by one, as shown here. They did this as efficiently as possible – making the Jews dig a mass grave first and killing them right on the edge of it, to cut down the work the soldiers had to do. Even so, this method of mass murder was not efficient enough for the Nazis. It was too slow, it used too much valuable ammunition (needed for the war) and it upset some of the soldiers who had to do it.

Death camps

The SS had already been experimenting in secret with mass murder. They had decided that some sort of gassing was quickest, cheapest and least upsetting for the murderers. Four death camps were set up: Chelmno, Belzec, Sobibor and Treblinka. As well as these camps there were also death camps built at the existing camps of Auschwitz and Majdanek.

The officials who ran the camps expected to process each **transport** of Jews within two hours. The camps had few barracks or other buildings – they did not need them. Most of the arrivals did not work, eat or sleep there. Only a few hundred 'work Jews' were left alive to keep things going. The **commandant** of Treblinka camp wrote to the Ministry of Transport on 28 July 1942, saying that the transports were bringing in 5000 Jews a day.

Auschwitz-Birkenau

Auschwitz-Birkenau was the death camp set up near the existing concentration and work camps of Auschwitz. Millions of '**undesirables**', most of them Jewish, were brought to the camp by train in cattle trucks. The trains brought them in through this entrance and stopped by a long platform, where the trucks were opened and the people unloaded. Sometimes they were all taken straight to the **gas chambers**. Sometimes some people were selected to live and work for a while. However, everyone sent to Auschwitz-Birkenau was simply waiting for his or her turn to be gassed.

The killing process

The Auschwitz State Museum has reconstructed a gas chamber at Auschwitz I, to show visitors how the process would have worked.

1 The people to be gassed were herded, naked, into a large, bare room, supposedly for a shower. Some rooms even had pipes and showerheads fixed up, to look more convincing.

2 The room had thick walls, and strong locks.

3 Zyklon B crystals, which gave off a poisonous gas, were poured either into the system of pipes and shower heads, or directly into the room, through holes in the ceiling, like the one shown here. Most people died within ten minutes, depending how close they were to the gas and how old or sick they were. The SS left the room shut up for 30 minutes, just to be sure everyone was dead.

4 The bodies were taken out and burned in **crematoria**.

Secrets

In Majdanek and Auschwitz, where death camps were attached to existing camps, the SS were told to keep the camps a secret. Anyone who stayed in these camps for any amount of time soon either worked out what was going on or was told by another prisoner or a **kapo**. Fania Fenelon asked the *kapo* in charge of her barracks what had happened to the people she had travelled with who had been loaded on to trucks marked with a red cross. At first, the *kapo* did not answer. Fania asked again and the *kapo* dragged her to the door:

' "Look ..." She pointed to a low building about 50 yards [46 metres] away, above which rose a chimney. "You see that smoke coming from that chimney over there? That's your friends, cooking." "All of them?" "All of them."'

Sonderkommando

Once people had been gassed the SS had the problem of disposing of the bodies. This was done by special units of Jewish men called *Sonderkommando*. They had to take people into the gas chambers and clear the gas chambers out afterwards. They had to check that no one was left alive. Then they had to strip the bodies removing anything of value from them, such as gold teeth. Then they had to dispose of the bodies. The dead had not been treated with any respect while they were alive – their bodies were not treated with any respect after death either.

Body disposal

There were so many bodies, thousands every day, that it was hard to dispose of them all. The SS tried piling the bodies into huge pits and covering them with lime to speed up the decomposition process. But the process was too slow, and took up too much space. It also left too much evidence behind. They also tried pouring fuel over the bodies and setting light to them, but this wasted fuel, which became more and more scarce during the war.

So the SS burned as many bodies as possible in crematoria. The death camps needed several crematoria, running all the time, to get rid of the bodies. Even then, they had a lot of ash from the bodies to dispose of. The ash was dumped in pits or lakes, or simply piled up to be disposed of later, when the 'Final Solution' had been completed and the death camps could be shut down.

Burning bodies

When Auschwitz-Birkenau was gassing the greatest number of people daily, the five crematoria could not cope with the numbers. At this time, and when a crematorium broke down, bodies were loaded into mass graves and burned. This photo was taken secretly by a *Sonderkommando* who then gave it to a Polish **political** prisoner, who managed to smuggle it out of the camp.

Leaving the camps

Some people were released from the camps. From 1933 to 1935 most prisoners were '**politicals**', and were released when the **Nazis** thought they would no longer be a threat to the Nazi state. Even then, they were watched.

A released 'political'
Walther P was released in September 1936 and went to live in Naumberg, Germany. He had to go to the local police station and sign a statement:

> 'I hereby submit my certificate of release from Lichtenburg concentration camp. I must report to the local police, criminal department, room 114, every Wednesday and Saturday at 11 o'clock. I shall do this punctually.'

On 28 April 1937 the Naumberg police sent a report to Berlin:

> 'Walther P has obeyed the police order to appear twice a week. He finds this extremely unpleasant and embarrassing. He has repeatedly asked to be released from it.

> 'P performs his job regularly and lives quietly. He has no contact with people who are suspected of hostility to the State. P is a member of the German Labour Front and is obviously trying to be part of the National Community. Further strict observation of P no longer seems necessary.'

AREA 12 GERMANY TERRORISM;CONCENTRATION CAMPS 1934.— RELEASE CERTIFICATE FROM THE CONCENTRATION CAMP HOHNSTEIN IN SAXONY STATE.

OES 736311

Released from Hohnstein

This is the release certificate of Otto Urban, who was in prison in Hohnstein camp, in Germany, from 29 November 1933 to 2 June 1934. All release documents had to have an official stamp and the signature of the camp **commandant**.

A released Jew
Some **Jewish** prisoners were released, before war broke out in September 1939. Herr Kahn was released from Buchenwald:

> 'We were shaved and our hair cut. An **SS** officer said he hoped we were rehabilitated and to prove it we should contribute to **Winter Aid**. A collecting box was produced and we all had to give something. We gave in, and paid ...

for "tickets" home. No one could leave until all had tickets. We were warned not to talk about our camp experiences, or we would be brought back and never get out alive. By the time we left it was 8 p.m.; we had been "processed" all day with no food. But we got away, after an 8 km (5 mile) walk to the station.'

Some prisoners managed to escape from the camps. Some escapees were caught, but others were not. The SS wanted prisoners to think that they would always be caught if they escaped. So they always claimed to have caught escapees and executed them. It had to look as if no one was getting away.

A successful escape

On 20 June 1942 four Polish prisoners escaped from Auschwitz I. They were working in the garage of the supply depot and managed to get hold of some SS uniforms. One dressed as a SS officer, two others as SS guards. The last one was dressed in his prison clothes and chains. In this way, they looked like SS men moving a prisoner from one camp to another. They stole a car from the garage and drove it 80 kilometres (50 miles) from the camp before abandoning it. They then sent the camp commandant a letter, jokingly apologizing for stealing the car. They were never caught.

Caught!

Hans Bonarewitz escaped from Mauthausen camp in June 1942, hiding in a wooden packing case on a truck driving out of the camp. He was caught eighteen days after he escaped. Hans was locked in a packing case like the one he escaped in, for a week, without food or water. The case was left in the square all that time, so the other prisoners could hear, and smell, his agony.

On 30 July he was taken out of the case, cleaned up and this photograph next to the packing case was taken by the SS. He was then executed in front of all the prisoners.

Safer inside?

Partisans fought the Nazis secretly, often hiding out in the forests. The Nazis knew about these groups and spent a lot of time trying to catch them. Not all of the groups would help everyone.

Roman Frister escaped from Starachowice camp one night when the camp lights were turned out during an air raid. Twenty-three prisoners made it into a nearby forest. They looked for, and found, a group of partisans to join. While Roman was at a stream, washing, the partisans killed the other escapees. They were Polish partisans who the Nazis left alone, because they hated Jews so much they killed any escapees. Roman went to a farm for help and was refused for fear of the partisans. Roman broke back into the camp and acted as if he had never tried to escape.

Going for help

Some prisoners not only escaped, they spread the news of what was happening in the camps to the outside world. Rudolf Vrba and Alfred Wetzler, both prisoners in Auschwitz camp, escaped in April 1944. They made their way to Czechoslovakia and told the Jewish leaders there how Jews from all over Europe were being killed in Auschwitz. Vrba had worked in the SS offices and had memorized the details of many of the people.

Shortly after they escaped two more escapees from Auschwitz arrived and confirmed what Vrba and Wetzler said. Their information was published in Allied newspapers and pressure was put on the Hungarian government to stop sending their Jewish people to Auschwitz. The **transports** stopped. The escapees saved over 170,000 Hungarian Jews.

Partisans

This photo shows some of the people who escaped to join a partisan group led by two brothers called Bielski.

Hidden from the SS

Israel Lau, a young prisoner in Buchenwald camp, was still alive when the SS decided to move the prisoners out ahead of the advancing American soldiers. The SS marched the prisoners out on 8 April 1945. Israel's brother, Naftali, hid Israel in a pile of dead bodies, telling him to stay there until the Americans arrived, which they did on 11 April. The soldiers found 21,000 people hiding with the unburied corpses. This shows what a huge number of dead there must have been. Naftali did not survive the march from Buchenwald.

Liberation

The last way to leave the camps was, simply, to survive long enough for Germany to lose the war. At that time the Allies, Germany's enemies, liberated the camps, letting the prisoners go. Most camps were **liberated** during April and May 1945. The Allied soldiers were stunned at what they found. They found more dead prisoners than living ones – the SS didn't want to leave survivors to talk about what had been going on. Other prisoners were liberated while being marched or transported by train to new camps.

Roman Frister

Roman Frister was born in Bielsko-Biala, Poland, in 1928. His father was a well-off lawyer. When the German army **occupied** Poland in 1939, the Fristers moved to Lvov, then to Cracow, where Roman's grandparents lived. The **Nazis** set up **ghettos** and ordered all **Jews** to move into them. Roman's grandparents, known Jews, had to go. Roman's father bought forged papers for the family and they stayed free, living in a small, damp basement room. Roman worked as a delivery boy, his mother later worked as a typist in a local **SS** Officers' Club.

Roman decided to get his grandparents out of the ghetto. Jews who had become Catholic were treated as Jews, but could be buried in Catholic cemeteries, outside the ghetto. Roman got his grandparents out disguised as a priest and a nun, with Roman as the priest's assistant. Roman put his grandparents on a bus to relatives in the countryside. Not long after, Roman was stopped by a patrol:

> 'I handed him my papers and, without being asked, also handed over my work permit ... There was a man lurking in a nearby doorway. The policeman holding my ID glanced at him and he nodded. "Jude" said the policeman.'

Roman was forced to lead the SS to his family. His father was sent to Plaszow concentration camp, just outside the city. His mother tried to save the family by telling an SS officer, Wilhelm Kunde, where all their property was in return for their lives. Kunde shot her and sent Roman to Plaszow, too.

Papers

An SS officer examines the papers of Jewish people in the Cracow Ghetto.

Epidemic diseases

Because of the poor living conditions in the ghettos, there were many outbreaks of disease. This notice, at the entrance to the Radom Ghetto, in Poland, warns people coming in of the dangers of disease. Once people were moved to camps, there were no warning signs like this. The Nazis did not provide people with enough access to clean water to stay clean and disease free.

Plaszow camp

Frister and his father were imprisoned in Plaszow camp first.

'One evening during the second week in the camp, the camp commander, Amon Goeth and the chief Jewish **kapo** came to our barracks. The kapo told us to hand over all our money or valuables; we had to fill Goeth's officer's cap, or else. The cap filled in half a minute. Goeth ordered the kapo to search a prisoner – there was money in his sock. Goeth shot him through the throat and looked around for his next victim. I was nearby, but the pistol passed me. He killed another prisoner, took his cap and left.'

Starachowice

In 1943 the Nazis decided to cut the size of Plaszow camp. Hundreds of prisoners were shot and thousands sent to other camps. By sheer chance, Roman and his father were put on the same train, to Starachowice:

'The camp was on top of a hill and other camps were scattered around nearby, their prisoners mostly a mixture of Poles and Jews. I was one of the youngest at the steelworks, making bomb casings and gun barrels. The steelwork furnaces worked around the clock and as long as they kept working we were allowed to live. My father's job was to push carts of steel mould ... Each cart weighed half a ton, and was always likely to come off the rails they ran on. When this happened, the guards beat the "guilty" worker until the cart was back on the rails.'

Roman's father caught typhus and died in hospital. Roman caught typhus, too, but survived. As the Russians closed in on Starachowice, the prisoners revolted. The camp was closed and the prisoners were sent to Auschwitz.

Auschwitz

The journey to Auschwitz was horrific:

'A sign in our cattle car said it held twelve horses or 24 cows. Now it held 100 men. It stank and was impossible to move. The doors of the car were opened on the third day ... we were on the "ramp" of Birkenau ... we were lucky – we were all marched off to the showers without a "**selection**". In the shower room we were ordered to undress, fold our clothes and lay them neatly at our feet. We were inspected by a young guard with a whip ... The prisoner on the right saw my bleeding leg and moved away as if I was a leper. The bloody bandage wrapped around it said: the boy dies. But the officer was distracted, chose to shoot another victim. So I lived.'

A huge camp

These photos show Auschwitz-Birkenau from the tower on the main gate. It stretches away as far as the eye can see in all directions. It took Roman some time to understand the camp.

'A view of the camp from the air would have showed a huge, flat, treeless stretch of land divided into rectangular strips. Each strip had about 20 barracks and a toilet block, surrounded by electrified fences. They were designed to keep the different sorts of prisoners apart, to make organized resistance harder ... Yet the Gypsies were kept in one section of the camp, all together, and were allowed to live as they pleased. The guards even let them go on playing their music after curfew, when the rest of us had to be in our bunks. Then, one night, I woke to silence. The Gypsies had been taken to the **gas chambers**.'

Taking a chance

Sometimes the SS came to the camp to look for replacement workers. Roman volunteered to work as a lathe operator – a job he knew nothing about. He was taken off to a steel plant in Auschwitz III:

'Now I would live while they had a use for me. But what would happen when I had to work my first lathe? In the morning we were kicked awake and kicked into line. We walked to the factory. At 6 a.m. I was faced with my first lathe. It bared its teeth at me, as if it was about to tear me apart. The foreman brought me a blueprint in German. I didn't understand the words or the diagrams. I looked around. The work force was huge. Dozens of machines stood in ruler-straight lines, each with an operator, each working. The foreman stepped up behind me, "Having trouble with the blueprint?"

[Roman] "No sir."

[foreman] "Your daily quota is 84 parts; anything over that you'll get extra rations, any less a whipping."

He moved on.

I took a metal rod and put it in the machine. I pressed a black button. Nothing happened. I pressed a red one. Nothing happened. The prisoner on my left said in Polish: "Hey yid, your God sure isn't going to work that lathe for you."

[Roman] "I suppose not."

[Polish prisoner] "You're not the first or the last to try this. Tomorrow they'll make soap out of you. You know that's what they do to dead Jews, don't you?"

[Roman] "At least I'll leave the world a cleaner place."

He liked the answer. Then he lent over studied the blueprint and showed me what to do. He set it up for me saying: "Everything here is automatic and very simple. Watch me closely." He taught me what to do. So I became a live lathe operator. His name was Kurt Kolonko and he saved my life.'

Giving out clothing

Clothing being given out at Mauthausen. The prisoners had to undress and re-dress in the yard. Even if they arrived in Mauthausen from another camp prisoners had to go through the whole arrivals process, including being issued with a different uniform.

Arrival at Mauthausen

In January 1945 the plant was shut down and evacuated. Roman was one of the prisoners taken to Mauthausen:

' "Let's go! Let's go!" yelled the Nazis. "Clothes off and against the wall, let's go!" I was out of my clothes in less than twenty seconds. The slowest had no space at the wall, and were beaten ... "Prepare for a shower!" We had come from Auschwitz, where the showers meant the gas chambers. Were the Nazis going to kill us? Not yet. Ice-cold water was sprayed from fire hoses aimed at our naked bodies. The powerful jet pounded my body, threw me against the wall. Blood ran down my face and froze there. The water had already turned to ice on my body. By the time they had finished there were dozens of corpses in the yard.

'We were herded through a gate into a second square. Here we were registered ... My bare feet were frozen to the ground. At last I was given a tin bracelet with my new number on it. "Guard it like gold," said the *kapo*. "You're a dead man without it." He gave me a kick in the direction of the showers. No, these were not gas chambers, either. Real water came out of them. I didn't notice it was boiling hot. That night, my body was covered in blisters ... Out of the shower I was thrown a shirt too small to button and trousers that were far too big. Jackets, we were told, were only for prisoners who had been here a while.'

Working

Frister nearly gave up in Mauthausen. No one was working in their part of the camp, and those who didn't work were more likely to be killed. Then he was taken to a sub-camp near Vienna that made tank engines:

'There were 1500 of us at morning **roll call**. The *kapos* and SS guards treated us less harshly, because they were told we had economic value. The food was still bad but we each had our own bunk with a straw mattress and a blanket ... It was easy to get used to these conditions.'

Death march

Then, one day there was a change:

'One roll call, instead of being sent to work, we were given a loaf of sticky black bread, a packet of red beet jam and a blanket. The camp **commandant** made a speech: "Prisoners! The **Third Reich** does not desert those who serve it, willingly or unwillingly. The Bolshevik hordes are nearing Vienna. We will march on foot to a safer destination, where you will work again." We marched in perfect formation through Vienna ... As we went the column fell apart. Prisoners fell behind, were left there. The SS didn't care anymore. After nine days hundreds of prisoners were missing and corpses lined the road. We arrived with 322 prisoners out of 1020.'

Frister ended up in a hospital ward again at Mauthausen, and was there when the camp was **liberated**. He became a journalist and emigrated to Israel in 1957. Frister became a reporter for the Israeli newspaper *Ha'aretz*. He published his autobiography, *Self Portrait with a Scar*, in 1993. It was translated into English as *The Cap, or the Price of a Life*, in 1999.

Surviving

These prisoners, who were photographed in Buchenwald camp after liberation, survived death marches and train evacuations. However, many prisoners were near death, from starvation, brutality and disease, when they were liberated. Soldiers and aid workers who arrived at liberation had to watch hundreds of prisoners die because they could not be saved.

Camps

This is a list of the main camps of several kinds in **Greater Germany** and Poland. Most of these camps are mentioned in the text, or appear on the map on page 5. The list does not include all of the sub-camps, prisoner-of-war camps or holding camps. Nor does it list camps in the rest of **occupied** Europe (for instance there was a camp as far away as on Alderney in the British Channel Islands).

Death camps
Belzec
Chelmno
Sobibor
Treblinka

Combined camps
Auschwitz-Birkenau
Majdanek

Concentration camps
Bergen-Belsen
Buchenwald
Dachau
Flossenbürg
Gross Rosen
Gunskirchen
Gusen
Lublin
Mauthausen
Natzweiler
Neuengamme
Ohrdruf
Sachsenhausen
   [Oranienburg]
Plaszow
Ravensbrück
Stutthof
Terezín [Theresienstadt]

Labour camps in Poland
Blizyn
Bochnia
Budzyn
Deblin
Gliwice
Izbica
Katowice
Koluszki
Mielec
Monowitz
Otoczno
Piotrkow
Poniatowa
Pustkow
Rzeszow
Skarzysko-Kamienna
Sosnowiec
Starachowice
Szebnie
Trawniki
Zawiercie

Labour camps in Germany
Bautzen
Braunschweig
Dora
Dresden
Flössberg
Hannover
Hessenthal
Krawinkel
Lieberose
Ludwigslust
Nordhausen
Rehmsdorf
Schlieben
Sonneberg
Spaichingen
Treglitz
Wiehagen

Timeline

1933

30 January	The **Nazi** Party comes to power in Germany. Adolf Hitler is elected Chancellor.
27 February	Fire breaks out at the Reichstag, the German Parliament. The Nazis blame German **Communists** for the fire.
28 February	German President Hindenburg's decree 'For the Protection of the People and the State, allows for the creation of concentration camps. The Nazis persuaded Hindenburg to pass the decree to fight what they called the 'Communist threat'.
17 March	**SS** set up, formed as Hitler's bodyguard
21 March	Dachau, the first Nazi concentration camp, set up. Concentration camps and labour camps set up steadily after this.
26 April	**Gestapo** formed
2 May	**Trade unions** banned in Germany
14 July	Political parties other than the Nazi Party banned in Germany

1934

20 April	Heinrich Himmler put in charge of the Gestapo
20 July	SS now in charge of their own affairs, not part of the army
2 August	Hitler makes himself *Führer*, sole leader of Germany

1935

15 September	Nuremberg Laws passed against German **Jews**

1936

29 March	SS has grown to 3500 men
17 June	Himmler put in charge of all police departments

1937

16 July	Buchenwald concentration camp set up

1938

13 March	Germany takes over Austria, which had once been part of Germany. The army marches in and the Austrian people vote to become part of Germany again.
8 August	Mauthausen concentration camp set up
9 November	*Kristallnacht*. Nazi-led violence against Jewish people: synagogues burned, shops and homes looted.
28 October	First Jews deported from Poland by the Polish government

1939

28 August	Rationing introduced. Covers food and essential items like clothes and petrol.
1 September	Germany invades Poland. Nazis begin to pass laws against Polish Jews. Soviet Union invades Poland from the east.
3 September	Britain and France declare war on Germany
28 September	Germany and the Soviet Union split Poland up between them
30 November	Soviet Union invades Finland

1940

12 February	First Jews forcibly removed from their homes in Germany and taken to **ghettos** in Poland
9 April	Germany invades Denmark and Norway
27 April	Himmler told to build a camp at Auschwitz
30 April	A large ghetto is set up in the Polish city of Lodz. All Jews from the city and the surrounding area are sent there. More ghettos are planned in other Polish cities for Polish Jews, and then for Jews from other lands.
10 May	Germany invades Belgium, France, Luxembourg and the Netherlands
15 November	Warsaw Ghetto set up

1941

6 April	Germany invades Yugoslavia and Greece
22 June	Germany invades the Soviet Union; mass executions of Jews as the German army moves through the Soviet Union
1 September	All German Jews over the age of 6 have to wear a yellow Star of David with '*Jude*' in black on it
From September	Mass gassings at Auschwitz begin with Soviet POWs and continue. They focus on Jews and become more regular from January 1942.
10 October	Terezin Ghetto set up; German and Czech Jews sent there.
16 October	Mass deportation of German Jews to Poland begins
28 October	10,000 Jews selected and killed at Kovno Ghetto, Poland
7 December	Japan bombs the US fleet at Pearl Harbor, bringing the USA into the war
8 December	First gassing of Jews, at Chelmno
11 December	Germany declares war on USA

1942

20 January	Wannsee Conference of the leading Nazis; outlines the 'Final Solution' to what the Nazis call the 'Jewish Problem'
21 January	United Partisan Organization, a Jewish resistance group, is set up in the Vilna Ghetto
1 March	First deportation of Jews from lands controlled by the Nazis to Sobibor death camp
17 March	First deportation of Jews to Belzec death camp
26 March	First deportations to Auschwitz-Birkenau and to the Majdanek death camp
27 March	First deportation of French Jews to Auschwitz
30 March–1 May	Bombing of Cologne
15 July	First deportation of Dutch Jews to Auschwitz
22 July	Daily deportations to Treblinka from the Warsaw Ghetto begin
4 October	Himmler orders that all Jews in concentration camps are to be sent to Auschwitz-Birkenau to be killed

1943

18 January	Four days of unrest in Warsaw Ghetto over deportations
17 March	Bulgaria, an ally of Germany, refuses to deport Bulgarian Jews
17 March	Hungary, an ally of Germany, refuses to deport Hungarian Jews
19 April	Warsaw Ghetto revolt begins
11 June	Himmler orders all remaining ghettos to be emptied and their inhabitants killed

1944

23 March	Deportation of Jews from Greece (occupied by the Germans) begins
9 April	Two Jews escape from Auschwitz and send news of the camp out of occupied Europe to the **Allies**. News of the camp cannot now be ignored.
15 May	Mass deportation and gassing of Hungarian Jews begins
From June	Death marches from camps in front of advancing Soviet troops
6 June	Allied troops land in Normandy, France
4 August	Anne Frank and her family arrested in Amsterdam. Anne's diaries of her experiences in hiding before this arrest became famous after the war.

1945

17 January	Final death march from Auschwitz-Birkenau
27 January	Soviet troops reach Auschwitz
11 April	US troops reach Buchenwald
15 April	British troops reach Belsen
29 April	US troops reach Dachau
30 April	Hitler commits suicide in Berlin, as the city is occupied by Soviet troops
5 May	US troops reach Mauthausen
7 May	Germany surrenders
20 November	Nuremberg trials of Nazi war criminals begin. First war criminals executed in October 1946.

Glossary

Allies used to mean the various countries that fought against Nazi Germany in the Second World War

Aryan used by the Nazis to mean people with northern European ancestors, without any ancestors from what they believed to be inferior races, such as Poles, Slavs or Jews. Aryans were usually blonde, blue-eyed and sturdy.

asocial Nazis called people 'asocial' if they did not support the Nazi state. Typically, they were drunks, people who would not work, homosexuals or members of a religious group whose beliefs might lead them to oppose the Nazis.

commandant person in charge of a camp

Communist person who believes that a country should be governed by the people of that country for the good of everyone in it. They believe private property is wrong – from owning a home to running a business. The state should own everything and run everything, providing the people with the things they need.

crematorium place with a special oven for burning bodies

Einsatzgruppen 'killing squad' sent in to the Soviet Union with the invading German army with the job of rounding up and killing as many Jewish people as possible

gas chambers large rooms that the Nazis filled with people. When the rooms were full the Nazis pumped poison gas into them, to kill the people inside.

Gestapo the secret police set up by the Nazis in 1933

ghetto an area of a town or city, walled or fenced off from the rest of the city, where Jewish people were forced to live

Greater Germany term used to mean the combined lands of Germany, Austria, Czechoslovakia and parts of Poland from 1939 to 1945. However, the Nazis also used it to mean all of the lands they controlled in Europe.

Holocaust in ancient times, the word 'Holocaust' meant 'an offering to the gods that was completely burnt away'. By medieval times it was used to mean 'a huge destruction or sacrifice'. From 1700 it was used to talk about the murder of large numbers of people. It is now mostly used to describe the deliberate attempt by the Nazis in Germany to destroy all the Jewish people in their power.

Jehovah's Witnesses a member of a religious group that was especially harshly treated by the Nazis because they refused to swear loyalty to Hitler

Jew (Jewish) someone who follows the Jewish faith. The Nazis also called people Jews if they had Jewish ancestors, even if they had changed their faith.

Judenfrei 'Jew Free' – a place with no Jewish people living there

kapo prisoner who is put in charge of other prisoners when they are working, making sure that they work hard

liberated used to mean a place, especially a camp, being freed from the control of the SS

lice small creatures that live on humans and bite them in order to feed

menorah seven-branched candlestick used in the Jewish religious festival of Hanukkah

Nazi the Nazi party is short for *Nationalsozialistische Deutsche Arbeiterpartei*: the National Socialist German Workers' Party

occupied used in this book to mean a country that has been captured by Germany and is ruled by Nazis supported by the German army

partisan someone who fights an army that has invaded and taken over their country

'political' person arrested for opposing Nazi idea or actions

propaganda information and ideas given to people in a way that will make them accept these ideas

quarantine medical word meaning keeping people who might be carrying a disease away from other people, in case they spread that disease. The term was used by the Nazis to talk about the first few days that people spent in a new camp. It was supposed to stop them spreading disease, but was really to terrorize them into obeying, so that they would not 'infect' the rest of the camp with ideas of escape or revolt.

race group of people with the same ancestors

Red Cross organization set up to give medical and other help in wartime or other times of crisis

Reich/Third Reich means empire. The Nazis saw their rule as the third German empire, with Hitler as the emperor, or *Führer*.

resettlement people are resettled when they are taken from the place they are living and working to live and work somewhere else

roll call count of all the prisoners in a camp, that took place morning and evening

sanitation providing clean water and removing waste and sewage to prevent disease

SS short for '*Schutzstaffel*' – security staff. The SS began as Hitler's personal guard. They ran concentration camps and death camps. They swore loyalty to Hitler, not Germany.

selection used to refer to the SS process in the camps of choosing people to kill

TB tuberculosis – an infectious disease, mostly of the lungs, which can be fatal

transport used to refer to a trainload of people being sent to the camps

'undesirables' used by the Nazis to mean any person that they did not approve of. People could be undesirable because of their political beliefs, race, religion or behaviour.

Winter Aid charity run by the Nazis to raise money to help the poor of Germany

Further reading

Auschwitz, Jane Shuter (Heinemann Library, 1999)
Diary of a Young Girl, Anne Frank (Penguin, 1997)
Ten Thousand Children: True stories Told by Children Who Escaped the Holocaust on the Kindertransport, Anne L Fox and Eva Abraham-Podietz (Behrman House, 1997)
The Past is Myself, Christabel Bielenberg (Chatto and Windus, 1984)

Sources

The author and Publishers gratefully acknowledge the publications from which written sources in the book are drawn. In some cases the wording or sentence structure has been simplified to make the material appropriate for a school readership.

All But My Life, Gerda Weissmann Klein (Indigo, 1997) pp. 15, 23
Auschwitz. A Doctor's Story, Lucie Adelsberger, translated by Susan Ray (Robson Books, 1996) p. 17
Auschwitz, Robert Jan van Pelt and Deborah Dwork (Yale University Press, 1996) p. 30
But I Survived, Tadeusz Sobolewicz translated by Witold Zbirohowski-Koscia (Oswiecim: Auschwitz State Museum, 1998) pp. 11, 21, 29
Chasing Shadows, Hugo Gryn (Viking, 2000) pp. 14, 19, 30
In Hitler's Germany, Bernt Engelmann, translated by Krishna Winston (Methuen, 1988) pp. 12, 38
In Memory's Kitchen: A Legacy From the Women of Terezín, edited by Cara DeSilva, translated by Bianca Steiner Brown (Jason Aronson, 1996) pp. 23
Nazism, 1919–1945, J. Noakes and G Pridham (University of Exeter Press, 1991) p. 38
Planet Dora, Yves Beon (Westview, 1997) pp. 22, 33
Playing For Time, Fania Fenelon, translated by Judith Landry (Syracuse University Press, 1997) pp. 16, 36
The Beautiful Days of My Youth, Ana Novac (Henry Holt, 1992) pp. 7, 8, 15, 16, 20, 23, 26, 27
The Boys, Gilbert, Martin (Weidenfeld and Nicholson, 1996) p. 41
The Cap: or the Price of a Life, Roman Frisker, translated by Hillel Halkin (Weidenfeld and Nicholson, 1999) pp. 40, 42–7
The Good Old Days: The Holocaust as Seen by its Perpetrators and Bystanders, edited by Ernst Klee, Willi Dressen and Volker Riess (Konecky and Konecky, 1991) pp. 13, 35

Places of interest and websites

Museums and exhibitions

There are lots of museums and exhibitions that you can visit to learn more about the Holocaust and see the evidence first hand.

Imperial War Museum
Lambeth Road, London SE16 6HZ
Tel: 020 7416 5320
Website: *http://www.iwm.org.uk*
The Imperial War Museum in London now has a permanent Holocaust exhibition.

London Jewish Museum
Raymond Burton House, 129-131 Albert Street, London NW1 7NB
Tel: 020 7284 1997
Website: *http://www.jewishmuseum.org.uk*
Or:
The Sternberg Centre, 80 East End Road, London N3 2SY
Tel: 020 8349 1143
The London Jewish Museum regularly features exhibitions and talks about the Holocaust.

Sydney Jewish Museum
146 Darlinghurst Road, Darlinghurst, NSW 2010
Tel: (02) 9360 7999
Website: *www.join.org.au/sydjmus/*
The Sydney Jewish Museum contains a permanent Holocaust exhibition, using survivors of the Holocaust as guides.

Websites

Before consulting any websites you need to know:

1 Almost all Holocaust websites have been designed for adult users. They can contain horrifying and upsetting information and pictures.
2 Some people wish to minimize the Holocaust, or even deny that it happened at all. Some of their websites pretend to be delivering unbiased facts and information. To be sure of getting accurate information it is always better to use an officially recognized site such as the ones listed below.

www.ushmm.org
This is the US Holocaust Memorial Museum site.

www.iwm.org.uk
The Imperial War Museum site. You can access Holocaust material from main page.

www.holocaust-history.org
This is the Holocaust History Project site.

www.auschwitz.dk
The Holocaust: Crimes, Heroes and Villains site.

http://motlc.wiesenthal.com
The Museum of Tolerance's Multimedia Learning Centre site.

Index